GLAMOURPUSS

CAT FITZPATRICK

TOPSIDE
HELIOTROPE

Topside Press
topsidepress.com
Some rights reserved. Most wrongs reversed.

Library of Congress Cataloging-in-Publication Data is available.

ISBN -- 978-1-62729-017-3

10 9 8 7 6 5 4 3 2

Author photo by Julieta Salgado
Cover photo by Susan Fitzpatrick
Cover design by Courtney Andujar
Website: courtneyandujar.com

For Ali.
Everybody advises you not to dedicate
your book to your lover, but what the hell,
I've never been much for good ideas

Wishes come true, not free.
-Stephen Sondheim

This isn't trauma, it's not even drama.
-Kristin Hersh

The joke is: it's not a joke.
-Annie Danger

To The Reader

Longing is weird; always at the periphery
Of your sight. Fate is very hard to change
Because you never know what you want.
Definitions attract me: I look back a lot.
Let me lay them out for you: My kisses,
Looks, desires, and all my other little wares

CONTENTS

Lullaby   15

Bright Lights   18

HEY NATURE GIRL!   20

Little Pure One   31

Six Women I'm Not   32
    Lavinia
    Grendel's Mother
    Eve
    Helen's Ghost
    Criseyde
    Penelope

Fucking Amy   38
    FUCK
    YOU
    AMY

How To Be Stealth   41
    Interview Clothes
    Phone Call
    Wine Tasting
    Bathroom
    Train
    Fag Break
    Targets
    New Breasts
    Headphones
    Boy Who Likes Me

Poems
Boy I Like
Monday
Computer
Car Park
Resignation

I Think You Are Like Water Love   47

All About My Mother   48

May Day   49
about the past
about turning nineteen
about friendship
about travelling
about my dick
about yahoo groups
about my cherry
about getting ready
about my iphoto library
about healing
about love
about stupid words
about gardening

Bon-Bons   62

All The Trans Girls Say   65

Enough Of This Oscar Peterson Shit   69

California Encomia   70
The Road, The Hills
Polar Bear
Truck Stop

The Goddess
The Oracle
Driving in

Ode To My Breast Implants   76

Grand Hotel   78

A Prayer To The Sun   86

Glamourpuss, Repent   87

Childless Poem   93

What Would I Do Without You   94

Damp and Regretful   96

Ubi Sunt   98

Blue Lipstick & Snowfall   99

Glamourpuss

poems by

Cat Fitzpatrick

Lullaby

1995

This room is full of terrors
My father lies in the next room
What is it that I'm doing in here
Dressing like a girl

There's my mother's clothes on racks here
Her low and soft lighting
What is it that I'm doing in here
Dressing like a girl

It is in my legs and fingers
It is in my stomach pit
That I can't stop coming in here
Dressing like a girl

But my father's out there dying
He is yellow, flat and thin
And his breaths are each unlikely
Grating like a rasp

I know where every drawer is
Where the tights and where the socks
Where the knickers, where the dresses
Hanging on the racks

This is not about her secrets
But I do know what they are
I've tried her wedding dress on
And her lacy underwear

Sometimes I get creative
With these bits of her old life
And imagine I'm these women
I'll never get to be

Like businesswoman, housewife,
Hostess at a ball
All of these old outfits
She never wears at all

Most times I touch my penis
And come wearing these clothes
Then hate myself so badly
Putting them away

This room is full of dreaming
It's full of hating everything.
It's full of sex and full of grossness
And full of not knowing

What my mother thinks I don't know
What she'll do when he is gone
What she needs from me I don't know
So I always get it wrong

I don't know what I'm doing in here
I don't know what it all means
My father's out there dying
And I'm dressing like a girl

I don't have a lot of time here
All my aunts will soon return
To keep watching for the dying
He will soon perform

I don't have time to be creative
And I don't know what I want
I'm just looking in the mirror
Getting in a state

I put on a pair of knickers
I pull out a random bra
It's not sexy it's not hopeful
But I know it's what I do

I go into the doorway
I look towards the bed
I give a little wave
Of greeting to my Dad

I whisper something stupid
'Hi' I say, 'I'm here'
I stand for thirty seconds
Not even full of fear

Just something, I don't know
I can't say what it is
I don't know what I'm doing
Standing in the door

I mean he's unconscious
In a day or two he'll die
He'll never know I stood there
Waved him goodbye.

Bright Lights

i.m. 'The Ghetto' Nightclub, Falconberg Court WC1

1

'Who wants coffee?' 'Fuck coffee. I want
A JD and coke.' Oh, take me dancing. Take

Me dancing now. 'A cigarette! Burn
A hole in my top. Tear my tights. I want

To look fucked up.' 'You are fucked up,' I do
Recall you said, 'Turn off the fairy lights.'

Then 'God, I love the streets. The dirty streets,
The lights on the main road. I love this town.'

Rum we brought in a diet coke bottle,
Drinking at the bus stop. Eyeliner.

2

In the queue, arrived too late again,
Don't know how to get a queue-jump pass.

At least an hour wait. It rains. We sing.
'Who's like us old friend? Damn few! Damn few!'

There must be eighty homos in this line,
Perhaps this is some kind of moral test.

Stares. Some girl is shouting about trannies.
A joke. So look away. 'One in, one out!'

'Who are these people leaving now? What fools.
Has no-one told them there's dancing inside?'

3

Disastered toilets, strewn with gossip, hair
And drugs. The bar's a press. 'Six Red Stripes please.'

Broken bottles crunch like salt put down
For snow. 'I popper-burnt my inner thigh!'

Everybody sweats. The boys remove
Their tops. I find my friends, I lose my friends,

I find my friends. 'He keeps hallucinating
Tables, trying to put his beer on them.'

'Stomp like a dinosaur!' Somewhere there's me.
Spinning. I am the only trans girl here.

4

And afterwards, outside, the air is grey,
It's suddenly cold and quiet, very calm,

Like the world just came onto the scene.
So I'm laughing, I want to start running,

'Did you see the girl all dressed in pleather?'
'What happened to that guy you kissed all night?'

Won't wear my coat, ticket machine won't work,
We'll walk, wet hair, and dazed. I see us walk

Back home. Smiling. 'It dries away the sweat,
And it's so great to watch the day begin.'

HEY NATURE GIRL!

This is meant to be a nature poem but
It starts in a railway station. There's me and there's
Two girls I know. That's three of us. Three girls.
The station has those ubiquitous ironwork
Ornaments that look as if they grew.
Like weeds, Perhaps that's nature too. I'm not
The one to ask. I'm very ill-prepared
For this: a week of walking across the North
Of England, along the wall, from sea to sea.

I have a borrowed sleeping bag and mat
And a new pair of walking shoes. I went
On a walk one time at school. My mother made
Me go; the other boys were horrible,
So it was just like all the time, but cold,
And wet, and you didn't get to leave at night.
I brought no food and seven books and all
The teachers laughed at me. The concept hikes
Might be for fun is very strange. But now
I'm bringing booze. And these two girls, let's call
Them Short and Horsey, are my actual friends.
It's different. When they asked 'You want to come
With us?' I said, 'You mean to walk three hundred
Miles, in drizzle, carrying all my stuff?
Of course! What dates?' I didn't hesitate.

And now it's now. I guess we should set out.
Turns out it's hard to leave Carlisle on foot.
I'd hoped for fewer dirty roundabouts.
OK I want this to be lyrical ,
I'm supposed to be getting in touch with beauty
    and nature,

What can I tell you about this roundabout?
It's round, it has yellow and black signs everywhere,
We nearly got killed crossing it with our stupid
Heavy bags, there was some grass in the centre
Which I guess is the first grass of the trip, so, yeah,
It's green (great description, dummy). At last
We leave Carlisle, there's fields, we get away
Up from the roads, which I'm sure must be a mistake,
But Short insists that she can read a map.
We hop across a stile, follow the hedge,
Away from the towns, towards the countryside.

Up one hill, down another, up and down.
My feet already hurt. It starts to rain,
But I'm prepared! My mother's given me
This fuchsia pac-a-mac she has from like
The eighties. Rolls up really small and light.
I whip it out, and feel proud, but then
I see the others putting on a whole
Array of gear, like plastic trousers, and things
That go over your pack. I didn't know
We needed them. My pack is getting wet.
My clothes and all my books are getting wet.
I panic. Horsey says she has bin bags
That maybe I could use. I try. They flap
And rattle in the wind, as if they hate
My guts, and long to bite or flee from me:
An angry beetle bin bag monster that
I've trapped, that doesn't want to help.
Both of the girls think it's hilarious,
I guess I do look pretty wild, but still,
It doesn't work. It leaks. My jacket leaks,
Because it's old. My shoes have soaked right through.
I trudge across the field towards some trees.

By night, the rain has lessened but hasn't stopped,
My fingers are wrinkled, even my knickers are wet.
We have to put up tents. Short turns to me,
And says 'Why don't you take the second one,
And me and Horsey will take this? You're taller,
So you should get the extra room.' 'I guess,'
I say, then 'thanks, of course.' They do their tent
So fast, and help me get my poles into
The holes. I know it's wet, I feel bad,
And so I say 'I'm fine from here.' They jump
Into their tent, I hear them giggling
Whilst I keep struggling with the pegs and ropes:
They shout encouragement from time to time.
My tent is all lopsided, the tension's wrong,
But I decide it's good enough for me.
I clump into the shower block to hang
My clothes. I've got a bottle of knock-off Aldi
Liqueur called 'Southern Belle' and I begin
To drink the sticky artificial stuff
Down on the fucking freezing concrete floor,
Willing my socks and shoes to dry somehow.

I'm drunk. I crawl into my wonky tent
And curl up. I wonder how Wordsworth dealt
With shit like this. He didn't have Goretex,
Just tweed. Old Wordsworth must have been quite tough,
I think. Tendentious so-and-so he was.

But ok morning's nice. There's dew, and birds
Singing, and all of that. And most of the clouds
Have gone. My head is very sore. Some cows
Are staring as we eat our packet food.
It tastes like cardboard stewed in mud. The cows
Are not like us. Their eyes are black and far
Apart, they have their thoughts and take their time,

At least, they chew as if they're having thoughts,
They look like aliens and Jesus aren't
They big? It could be worse, they could be men,
I say, because we are a group of girls.

OK so then we'll walk! More fields more mud,
Increasingly more hills. There are some flowers
Under the hedges, hiding here and there.
The birds don't come too close, it's mostly sheep.
The sky is nice, I like the sky, it moves;
I guess I like how plain the landscape is.
My bag weighs half as much as me since all
My clothes are damp, but you get used to it,
Though people say that about everything.

We're not alone - there's lots of ramblers here,
Though most are old, the men with grizzled beards,
The women in their tasteful fleecy coats,
Lilac, pastel pink, aquamarine
(I'm envious of them: my fleece is black)
Dotting the landscape as I look ahead,
Like hardy flowers blooming by the paths.
They pay to have their bags driven from pub
To pub ahead of them, by men with vans,
Who advertise under the name of 'sherpas'.
They look so free, they are so sensible
So comfortable, they know the way to go,
They probably know all the trees
By name. They nod at us as we tramp past,
Sometimes they stop to talk about the weather,
Or tell us stories of their distant youth.
They make me nervous, don't know why. It's not
That I'm afraid they'll think that I'm a boy,
Without my makeup, skirts, and heels, and all
Those unambiguous accessories.

I mean, they might, but that's not all, that's not
The only way I feel like a fraud,
Out here among this nature and Englishness.

Whatever. Let's do this thing! I bet I can
Get up this slope faster than that old bloke
For all his lightweight hiking poles. Faster
Than Short and Horsey, who say they want to stroll
And 'see the views'. Well sod the view,
Slowpokes, I'm speedier than you! I'm way
More out of breath. I have to stop, I won't,
This hill looked shorter down below but now
Each time I think I'm near the top, it curves
To show another bit of slope. Just to
The fence then rest. Can we have lunch? Please give
Me lunch and is there still some Southern Belle?

Oh god yes bargain booze and processed cheese
And beans. We gorge, and Horsey makes
A medal out of string and Laughing Cow
Container that she hangs around my neck,
Because I am a laughing cow, she says.
I pose for photos by a hawthorn tree
In bloom, then find a stick and stomp away
Across the verdant hills bedecked like this,
With scudding clouds above, and muddy feet:
Some kind of avatar of foolery,
Poorly prepared, a bit embarrassing
Ungainly, noisy, full of eagerness,
Blazing across this dignified landscape.

Another night. My tent still leans in ways
That break the laws of gravity. But then,
Gravity's never been a strength of mine
(As Horsey made so clear). It trips me up.

I've fallen I don't know how many times
This walk, and sprained my ankle twice because
These shoes don't offer the support of boots
(Which I suppose I should have bought instead).
I snuggle deeper in my sleeping bag
And listen to the wind. I always make
All these mistakes. Always. You know, I know,
I'll never be a serious person like you.
Watch me fall and get back up again.
No-one ever wants to sleep with me.

We see the wall, the fort at Birdoswald
The bridge at Willowford (what's left of it)
This stuff is OLD. The Romans did this thing,
They built it all in just six years, and now,
Well, mostly it's dilapidated but
It isn't gone. Foundations, bits of walls,
You can imagine it: A roman camp!
Seeing this stuff reminds me of the trips
My dad adored taking my family on.
I used to climb on all the ancient stuff,
And I still do, though Short does not approve.
'Catherine, you'll damage it!' she hisses at me,
And so I stop, and try to act mature.

They have these shoes and ancient letters that
They dug out of the mud beneath the fort
There's party invitations and little notes
From nineteen-hundred years ago. They have
The first handwriting that we're sure is by
A woman anywhere in Europe. Wow.
It's strange to think of Romans having friends,
Hanging out. The stories you get told
Are all about this tiny set of men,
Sometimes their slaves and girlfriends. But there were

A load of Romans. And they lived all kinds
Of lives. What would someone like me have done?
What words could I have written to my friends?
Which friends? I can't imagine reading those.
I barely know how to communicate
Or what to say about myself today.

It's nice to be on holiday with girls,
We are a three. I know it should be four,
Like on TV, but still, I have girl friends.
Sometimes I count the entries in my phone
To check I know more girls than boys. I do.
Which reassures me. Girls are friends with girls,
And Short and Horsey are almost old friends.

We met in our first year at uni, back
Before I was a girl. But they were nice
About that stuff. Horsey is loud, though not
As loud as me (I try to be muted
but I forget) and works in a 'boutique',
But owns a flat her parents bought. She's fun,
She always has the nicest clothes, I wish
They fit so I could borrow them. She used
To ride horses – one time when we were drunk
I wound her up by claiming that she did
Gymkhana. She kept on saying 'No,
It's Pony Club!' Apparently they're not
The same, and Pony Club is better. Short
Is much more serious, and always acts
All well-behaved – at least until she drinks.
When she is drunk she gets mischevious
And wants to steal things and crash weddings
And pee in alleyways (which I will never
Do). She sleeps around a lot (I'm like,
How does she find these boys? I never can)

She is becoming a psychiatrist
And always wears flat shoes and cardigans.

So anyway these are my closest friends.

We drink. We finish off the booze we brought,
And head towards the pub. A gourmet pub,
Out here! It's all oak beams and nooks and snugs,
It seems almost as ancient as the hills
Outside. I get a pint of real ale,
The others order G&Ts. Should I
Have had a gin? But girls can order pints;
There are some other women here with pints.
Before she's had hardly a sip Short says
She feels sick and that she's going back.
We ask if we should come, she says she's fine,
So her and Horsey hug, she waves to me, ⟵
I say 'try not to die' and 'can I drink
Your gin?' and then I order cabbage leaves
With pesto stuffing and butternut velouté.

And so we get fucked up, and then argue
About the NHS (I wish I could
Let go of arguments, I get so stuck,
Having opinions makes me feel sick)
And for a second it seems the night's gone wrong
But then we start to laugh about this time
A guy in a trucker hat was hitting on
Short in this bar, and we kept singing *Keep
On Truckin* (OK, mostly Horsey sang)
And he had no idea, ha men are dumb,
She says, and I'm so glad I'm not a man.

And then we're walking back, the darkness is
Intense. It's not like cities, here there is

No light. You cannot see your feet, and I
Am somewhat drunk and didn't bring a torch.
Oh inky night you cover up so much!
It doesn't matter if I fall or walk
Into a bush (though Horsey laughs at that)
You are a difficult but peaceful state,
When nobody can see the way I look.

It turns out Short has had the runs, she's still
Awake, or rather up and down. Our torches
Light her up as pale as a sheet.
She says she thinks Horsey should sleep with me,
Because she doesn't want to make her sick,
So Horsey says ok, but could I wait
Outside while she puts her pajamas on.
Which, like, that's fine, I go a little way
And sit down on a rock and have a fag
And stare up at the stars, and think how nuts
It is that they're so far, it is so big.
And even that there is a universe at all –
That being is – is weird: it is uncanny that
There is reality, including me
Right here, and maybe it's less weird that I'm
(I hear Short running to the loo again)
Transsexual if everything is strange.

When I get back Horsey is in her bag,
Already dozing off, facing the wall.
I get in mine and say 'don't let the bed
Bugs bite' and as I fall asleep I think
That really this has been a lovely night,
The kind of thing that being young is for.
I am so grateful that I have such friends,
I am so lucky to be friends with them.

It isn't wild here. I mean it's bleak,
But this is occupied. It's all in use,
The moody farms, the turfy valleys and
The yellow hills, the lines of drystone walls
Dividing up their slopes, so people know
Just who has what and whose those sheep there are,
The churches, villages and careful clumps
Of woods. This isn't any wilderness,
I know, but as we cross it step by step,
I come to think that I'm in something that
Is Nature. That's the only word I have:
Cities are part of us, big as they are,
But here, convenient though we have made
It be, we are a part of something else.
I want to feel that way. I mean, I know
I'm not like other people. I know that too.

Footsoreness starts to be a comfort, bag
Becomes a task I do for fun. I'm used to it.
I start to think maybe it's fine that I
Don't know the names of any plants: the point
Is not to know but just to move. Then we
Get lost. I don't know when it is we jump
A stile too soon, or wander off the path,
But soon we come into a patch of woods
And end up following a stream downhill:
The compass says this can't be right.
We turn and clamber upwards through the ferns,
It's steep, we've lost our way and it's okay,
Somehow. We crest the ridge and leave the woods
And come up to a gate into this high
And quiet field, set-aside for hay.
There are no other hikers here, there's trees
All round, just sky above, hardly a noise.
It feels okay to stop and even think a bit.

And so it strikes me suddenly and hard:
I am a fucking tranny standing in
A field, what the fuck? I thought my kind
Was meant to hide in cities, hanging out
In dirty bars, or staying home to cry.
Someone like me, I am unnatural and
Ungracious, lumpen, clumsy, weirdly-shaped,
what am I doing in the countryside?
We're never hiking on TV, no-one
Believes we might do something so mundane
And nice, but really nature isn't nice
Although we sometimes make it look that way.
It's not normal. I've found a secret place,
Some kind of plateau. Nature doesn't care.
Through this gate, the grass, the slanting light,
Maybe a sluggish bee or two. No-one
Can see me as I stop and look and let
The others walk on down the path ahead.

Little Pure One

Little pure one
Wants to occupy
A space of clarity

Wants to be moral
And coherent
Wants to disappear

Six Women I'm Not

meditations on having sex with straight men
who don't know you're trans whilst pretending
to be a literary character

Lavinia

I thought I'd never talk again: It seemed
I lost my speech when I received these scars.
They threatened to disclose so much about
My past, but I kept dumb. Well, if I'd talked
I would have only cursed myself: 'Your fault,
You bitch, it's all your fault' or 'Hide your shame
From view, you heavy hairy flesh-and-bone,
Your skin shows up the truth, you'll always be
A man' or such. Self-hatred for self-love,
And what's the good in that? At nights I kept
The tears and ululations down. But now,
Enough. Nobody made me anything,
And if you'd kiss me then you'd find I have
A tongue that's getting ready for to speak.

Grendel's Mother

If I've been set apart, then where's the mark?
I mean, ok, I've got this love-bite on
My neck, but he has no idea, I think.
We're by the water watching sunset leave,
And holding hands. I guess I'm holding back.
You might call that a choice, but if I left
(I will leave, I won't call) and swum into
The sea, out past the fires on the oil
Refineries and underneath the waves,
Down to a secret place, to wait, afraid,
Until some hero came to kill or kiss
Me, then I'd accept our curse. I may not stay
With him, but when I'm done I'll go and get
Another drink, and try to keep my head.

Eve

Bittersweet? Oh, I'm sorry. Talk to me,
All ignorance, about the things we'll do.
What should I say? I've tried to tell myself
That there's no harm in it, and sure as hell
I wish I'd some desire for him to fall
In with, but here, as elsewhere, when I should
Be lips to lips, bright eyes, I find I feel
Ashamed to own my nakedness, to bear
His look. My vagina's almost a work
Of art. I should be proud. Oh, innocence,
The things that you don't know! He wonders why
I taste so sweet. Sweetness, that's lubricant,
And not my nature. Wonder why I'm bitter?
Bite the apple. I never asked for this.

Helen's Ghost

As if I come from long ago, or far
Away, self-consciously, I dress and do
My face and show myself, so eager that
I grasp at every little touch I get.
What carnal substance can I conjure up?
Am I enchanting? Can I haunt your dreams?
Some secret knowledge this: Will you screw me?
Of course he will. And so the bargain goes:
He calls me up, I come; I take a risk
On my appearance, unbecoming flesh
Mixed up with spirit; I catch onto his breath,
Return his kiss, as if his lust might then
Inspire or quicken me, as if somehow
He'd draw me a new body on his lips.

Criseyde

Bite me! Bite me! Pull my hair. Hold me
Against the bed, and let me struggle, and
Then stop! and then softly again: just trail
Your lips and fingers, take some time with me.
I can perform positions till the sun
Comes up on us. I have rehearsed this show.
Next we'll lie down, the curtains drawn,
And then he'll fall asleep. And then I'll go.
Faithless? He courted me. I have to leave
Behind my shame, that past in which I have
No place, and learn to get by as I can.
I made no promises to him and told
The lies I needed to, no more. I'm not
Untrue. And all I'm taking is my time.

Penelope

Here, in between of sleep and waking up,
Feet first, I find my room all full of day:
I've washed up on my bed, and now the sun
Is drying off my dreams, warm sheets for sand,
On what I see is that familiar shore
Where I've been drawing out my threads, these years,
Spinning my stories and unpicking them.
These years, weaving a body out of words,
Unravelling it again, as if my life
Were just material, as if I'd get
It right sometime. What if some man came back
And took my hand and said 'it's me'? I am
Not her. We none of us can be like them.
None of these stories do us any good.

Fucking Amy

FUCK
Fuck you Amy you are a pain in the ass
Why do we have to sleep on the couch
Why won't you let me touch you more
What does it take to make you smile?

Listen shut up you ARE pretty
I actually do think you're beautiful
Bony body narrow arms
Thailand vagina I know it's shallow
But I like to put my fingers in it

Of course I know we're breaking up
I know we are never getting back together
I know you are a fucking nutcase
But I'm still in love with you alright?

YOU
Never fuck another trans woman
They are all crazy bitches
They bite scratch hide hate things
Just like I do oh my god

Why are we all so hurt so angry?
I wish I knew a way to heal
Either of us I wish you could
Forgive me for being one of us
I wish my love meant healing too

Whatever Amy I've had enough
I wanted a dramatic affair
You wanted to turn someone down
We both got what we wanted from this

AMY

Amy it was a long time ago now
I haven't talked to you in years
You were too intense I can't forget
But I don't know what the hell it was

You remember at my mum's house that time
We were staying there alone
And we got naked by the fireplace?
You let me touch your lovely cunt
And you came suddenly and then cried

I'm sorry I'm not cis I'm sorry you're not
Ok fuck that I'm not sorry at all
I wish it didn't have to be this way
But I don't know how it could have changed

How To Be Stealth

whilst holding down a job in telemarketing

Interview Clothes
It is a journey there, first time. Three trains, then a walk.
I call my mother to tell her that I'm going to
An interview. She asks me what the job will pay,
What it involves. I lie and say I'm not quite sure.
I'm wearing my trouser suit, and the pointy scarlet heels
That pinch my toes with the bow on the front. I cross the road
Towards a yellow metal building and try to ignore
My hangover. I'm twenty-three and I feel like such an adult.

Phone Call
You've only got your voice. 'Helloo I'm Catherine from
Your Club for Wine, I have some offers just too good
To go into our brochures' I emphasise my name.
He says 'Young man'. I don't react. This is my task:
To keep them on the phone until they buy to make
Me stop. Don't sound upset. My boss says someone's always
Getting sold. So I am working on my voice.

Wine Tasting
There's always a bottle or two to try. We have
To know the product. We discuss it sagely, in depth,
Starting at 10 am each day. There's a lot to learn.
I could become a buyer if I pass the exams.
I could be the next Jancis Robinson!
She wins awards and puts out books and gets to go

To banquets at the Chateau du Clos de Vougeot
And has a thing she's doing with her life. And she
Looks sort of bony, like she might be trans. Although
I googled her, she went to a women's college, she's not.

Bathroom
It's halfway through the call I think Oh fuck I don't
Know where the letter is! It came this morning to
Announce I'm legally a girl, at last. I read
It on the train and cried, then here I read it in
The loo and cried again and wiped my face and washed
My hands. I must have left it by the sink. And now
They'll read it and they'll know. I almost faint but then
Instead I sell a case of Sauvignon and walk
(Don't run, don't run) and there it is. It looks untouched.

Train
The doors have closed, I've missed my stop. There's nothing I
Can do: I guess I'll just stay late. Next station's small,
There's no-one there, it's summer, I leave and crawl under
A hedge and stretch out in a field in the sun. There's warmth
And flowers and butterflies. Platonic England, I think,
As if I still did shit like this. It seems to be
A while until I hear the train and have to go.

Fag Break
Alyssa offers me Reiki. She says it's her passion. James
Is scheming to make a fortune. His hair is shiny and neat.
I talk about poems. How did we all get involved in this?

Targets

I meet the targets every time. You have to be
Ruthless. The people you call are resources. Numbers. Of course
I want them to like their wine. Whatever, wine is great.
And once you're done you get to leave. These are and aren't
Relationships. Perhaps they wouldn't even care.

New Breasts

I wear a high-necked top, and hope that hides the change.
It's stripy and pretty loose. I hate how it looks but I think
Nobody notices my boobs. Of course, I'm wrong.

Headphones

The Goldberg Variations. I like the Andras Schiff
Recording. It sounds so effortless, so self-involved.
The first is how it would be to be blessed. Yes, some
Are sad, like number twenty-five, so-called 'black pearl',
But still all clear and light. They make me feel free,
As if my days were happening to someone else,
Already memories, inevitable, full
Of meaning, lit up from within, moving like art.
Although I can't imagine what the meaning is.
Today I don't communicate with either of
The boys who share my ride. I keep my headphones on.

Boy Who Likes Me (Nick)

I mean, he's pathetic. He's always trying to be nice to me.
He always agrees with things I say. He sits by me
And tells me jokes. He's nerdy, beardy, round and short.
We talk about Riesling, and also sometimes Chenin Blanc.
We're sort of friends. Later, when everything's gone wrong,

I'll start screaming at him that everyone can see
That I'm transsexual and now I have to die,
And he will say it doesn't matter, that I am
A beautiful woman, or something fucking dumb like that.

Poems

At home I write about how I can't imagine or
Inhabit my body. It's winter. All I am is attempts
To predict and meet your expectations. My gender is what
Do you think you're seeing today? In my poems I live in a desert
And there's nobody there but me. My flatmate leaves and
  I don't care.
I go to gay clubs and pretend I'm someone's straight best friend.
I throw a lot of dinner parties. I'm always drunk.
The employee discount is my favourite thing about this job.

Boy I Like (Tom)

He's stocky and blonde and grins like he knows everything,
And he's great at selling. Always slightly ahead in the stats.
He has an open relationship, so I pursue
Them both. At their flat I try to play footsie with his wife;
When she goes to bed, and I sit up and drink with him.
He tells me he used to be a chef and demonstrates
The proper way to poach an egg. Another night
Like this, when I am not expecting it at all,
He is the one who tells me they all know I'm trans.
Or like, there's not unanimous accord on it,
But there's been talk and he (of course) is sure. He says
He knew the second that we met. Although I cry,
Although I implore him desperately, he can't explain
This insight of which he is so proud. On Monday I'll still
Have to meet his gaze and say hello. I'll have
To meet everyone's gaze and pick up the fucking phone.

44

Monday

I meet everyone's gaze and pick up the fucking phone.
I don't control my thoughts but I control my face.
It's a good day, if what you're asking me about
Is how much shitty wine I force people to buy.

Computer

It has its programs: dialler, targets, offers list.
It's never tired. Never even gets turned off.
Every morning it's there. It says: Call them, call them
Ask them do they need some wine then lie the way
I prompt you to until they buy or else hang up.
It is my frenemy. I cover it with drawings I do
Of skulls, and little cartoons of people who hate their lives.
I dance around the office and offer a single page
Of Blake to everyone: Songs of Experience.
I know they know, but apart from Nick, who I finally kiss,
I never mention it to anyone at all.

Car Park

They have this model wine press in the parking lot.
Full size. I'm inside, calling my mother on the phone
And saying this can't go on. I do not tell her that
They know I'm trans, or that I'm living alone again
Eating odd times, crying to Ryan Adams songs,
And getting near the bottom of my overdraft.
I do not say my understanding of myself
Is a dead end, I can't be normal, it doesn't work.
Instead I say perhaps this isn't the right career
For me, perhaps I'm not cut out for an office job,
Sorry. Inside the tun, against the cheap oak planks,
Peering through the gaps, ready to turn and run.

Resignation

I'm never going to Theale again. I almost want
To give up wine. All I did was lose and lose.

I Think You Are Like Water Love

So then maybe to see you is a drink,
A jug poured over me,
Or else to swim.

Perhaps from off the rocks where I had been
Stretched in the heat I came
And jumped in you

And found you cool and strong and green, a lake
So deep, I hadn't known
How deep it is.

All About My Mother

My mother has very tiny eyes:
It took me years to notice this.
Hardly any white at all
Between the pupil and the lid.
The day I saw how small they were,
I was transformed. I wondered who
This unknown woman standing in
The lift with me and talking was.
Looking at me with her little eyes,
As if my mother was still around,
As if I wasn't all alone
At last, as if my past was still
The past it used to be, before.

May Day

thirteen sonnets, twelve years too late

about the past
What do you do after twelve years? Recall?
Then fuck, I was eighteen and had no friends,
And I was *crazy*, thoughts like: must get out
I hate my skin, just shut up shithead just

Be quiet, NO, I have some words to write,
I'll run outside, the cold is free, I want
My fingers to go numb I can't be still —
Alright! So don't recall if it's like that.

I left this suffering behind me years
Ago. Let it be dead. I'm over it.
So over all those sonnets that I used

To write. Dramatic, maudlin, structureless.
Why am I writing more? As if I miss
The past. As if I had a use for it.

about turning nineteen

Well, everything was simple then.
Perhaps that's what I've lost. My school was boys,
They hated me on sight, eleven years,
Until I left for uni. That was clear.

Even the way I felt when I had made
A *friend*, a *girl*, who for my birthday gave
Me weed and nail varnish as a joke:
It was so simple. Put it on, get high,

And go outside. I wonder what I said?
Probably babbled, asked her fifteen times
'Is this ok?' So young and desperate, which

You know is code for hope. I don't need that.
Fuck clarity. Fuck simple desperate girls,
And misery. Fuck how it has to be.

about friendship

OK so it's the story of my life
In sonnets. *What I Learnt from Pain*. Or else
Transitioning for Idiots. 'I long
To be girl, will you believe me please?'

By which I meant, I hope you'll validate
My weird importunate desire with
Your normal eyes and words. Or else, 'Hey Guys!
I bought some wine. Come on! Par-taaay?' Which meant

The same. I hardly speak to them these days,
Those *friends* I courted so attentively.
I left. Hell, it's their fault. They never did

Say 'yes'. And here, I'm longing for the chance
To care what someone thinks. I haven't learnt.
When did I ever even think at all?

about travelling
At least, admit it wasn't all like that.
Like when I told my mum. She said it was
A phase and selfish, that I couldn't be
At home and dressed that way. I called this boy

I'd met, and picked an outfit for the train:
Beige skirt and boots and turtleneck and shades.
I had a sense of *glamour,* was so *bright,*
Brought whisky, talked too much: 'I have ideas,

Can we stay up and ask what beauty is
And am I clever (do you love me back?)
And did those people realise I am trans?'

What I remember clearest is the light,
Lamplight, the mornings walking to the pub.
It was unbalanced, but he took me in.

about my dick
And now at last it's time for me to talk
About the fact my mother paid to chop
It off. Yes, I'm a lucky one. The food
Was good, the view was beautiful, it was

So civilised. The surgeon said I was
Too young but since I had a 'good degree'
He'd take a chance. And I was full of thanks.
It took me years to work out how to cum.

My dick still turns up in my dreams. I know
That worried me. I think I had to try
Too hard. I had to treat a *choice* as *proof*.

I am so angry at those men. I guess
I can admit I like the thing they did,
Or at the least, decide that it is mine.
.

about yahoo groups

I bet I have those posts. I'm too ashamed
To look. I bet they're all just lists of ways
I knew I was a girl. Like, I was friends
With girls at school. Also I liked Care Bears.

Or else confessing how I wore my Mum's
Dresses and wanked. I thought I was so brave.
Oh god, the ones about neurology!
But we were talking. Even that was new,

For me. The world said that we were gross,
I can't forgive myself for listening.
Although this sonnet's making all the same

Mistakes: *I've got it all worked out at last!*
Perhaps I'm just afraid if I re-read
Those posts, that it would make me fucking sad.

about my cherry
I drunk a bottleful of vodka and
He took my top off where I had no breasts.
We got into my bed. He said 'You're scared.'
I was. Is that like lust? And then he left

And Oh my God I kind of had some sex
I'm so hung-over but I need to call
My *friends* and gossip over brunch as if
I'm on TV. I need to fall for him

And follow him around for months. Of course
He never kisses me again. I do
Receive a note, years on, lamenting that

His wife is pregnant. He implies he thinks
He missed a chance with me, oh wild youth.
There's no apology. He's not that smart.

about getting ready
I put so much *confixor* in my hair,
It crisped. I'd make it to the mirror by
The door (who has a mirror by the *door*?)
And I'd freak out. I'd change my shoes six times,

My dresses eight, to get it right. I aimed
To look as if I knew what it was like
To know what all the things you want to be
Are like. I think that I looked better then.

I know I worked so hard, I ought to have.
Perhaps I'm losing it. Not just my fear.
My poise and dash. I have nothing to prove,

I say, but that self-hatred was itself
A terrible adventure. How alive,
How beautifully composed my panic was.

about my iphoto library

These selfies. I still look at them sometimes.
Their meaning hasn't emptied all the way.
I'm crying. See my tears, my wailing mouth?
I made them years ago to show myself

That any hope is just a trap, which has
To die. It doesn't matter (so I sobbed)
Whether you pass or not, you still turn out
To be this stupid lonely weeping thing.

And what I said is true. You cannot change
Your self into another self. I tried,
And people always made that clear to me.

I learnt that fact. But what a lesson. How
Can that be what I think, who used to say
To everybody, I'm an optimist?

about healing

I have been writing these things thirteen years.
I ought to be better at it by now.
What use does any of this have? I just
Got older, cried and drunk, got fucked,

Had a good time, bad time, whatever, had
A time and now I think it needs to have
A use? Well you know how it is. Who wants
Us? No, you're *still* not like we are. It seemed

I was *transitioning*. Is it done yet?
I asked. It seemed the thing to say.
I worked to be somebody else. And now

I am, it seems I want to change my mind.
As if I could redeem that past instead
Of simply screeching *Memory! Revenge!*

about love
And obviously life goes on. She thinks
I'm sexy. Yes, I know it isn't easy to
Believe. At first I couldn't cope with it,
I had to get away out of the bed,

It is unsafe, there's no way it will work,
I'll hurt her, here I go, just so she quits
This stupid loving me I cannot use,
And lets me act like I am bodiless.

Turns out your body never goes away.
Stop crouching shaking in the corner. Breathe,
Go back and touch your clit. If I just rub

Enough, I'm bound to come. So nothing can
Be changed. But there is still the future and
In mine I'm gonna have to learn to screw.

about stupid words
I ask, how do you meet that person that
You were? Say, Let's go dancing let's go have
A drink and you can tell me all of your
Secrets? I wouldn't understand a word

She said, although it broke my heart. Perhaps
On her behalf, some righteous anger has
It's place. And who gets anger? Everyone.
Will it be righteous? Maybe not. So then

Compassion? Younger me, it's with such grace
You seem to move. Insouciance. Or Joy.
I grieve your loss, your possibility,

My bitterness. What good is that? What can
I offer you? I guess I dream that if
I say it right it will have been worthwhile.

about gardening
And so from all of this ferocity
I've gone and made an ill-proportioned group
Of passionate and broken sonnets, like
I think that helps. But there's no saving her.

Then what? Say I remember, say I call
To mind, me dancing in Poptastic, by
The fan, or drinking by the library
(That posh red wine) or running down the street

In dungarees? You only keep it all,
Or lose it, otherwise. Maybe I learnt,
I don't know what. Forgot some stuff. It's May.

I have the radio, this sweater that
I like, and dirty nails. Here I am,
Still just as blue-eyed, dumb and full of beans.

Bon-Bons

'sticky and sweet'

No money left.
I have no gifts,
except for this:

These words that fall
So easily
Out of my mouth.

*

The way you smell.
Never too much.
Instead of fate

I might believe
In this. Like milk,
Like earth, like grass.

*

Those games we play
Where you convince
Me things are true

That aren't make me
So happy that
I don't know what.

*

You concentrate
So hard on things.
It makes you sweet.

Even your rage
Fills my heart
With tenderness.

*

How can it be
That I always
Want more of you?

Are you holding
Something back?
Or is it me?

*

Our bodies are
Peculiar.
We made ourselves

Into a pair
The best we could
With what we had.

*

Please take my head
Into the place
Beside your breasts,

Beneath your arm,
And hold me there
Until I move.

*

Those times you love
Me are so good.
I know that you

Prefer it when
I am direct.
So here, I tried.

*

All The Trans Girls Say

When I first transitioned I didn't know any trans women
I didn't even know anyone else who knew any trans women
I swear it's the truth not one I walked around the medieval towers
And secret lawns and felt just like the biggest freak on earth
So grateful for every bit of condescension I could get
And crying out do you believe that I'm a real girl
Like all the trans girls say

La, la-la-la la-la la

At last I saw this psychiatrist this was two years later
He sent me to Laura she'd been in the navy become a lawyer faced
Discrimination she gave me wine she couldn't pull the cork
This made her smile not as strong since the estrogen she said
She'd been on awful dates in hotels but now she had a man
They had a normal happy life we never spoke again
Like all the trans girls say

La, la-la-la la-la la

I wandered the empty world like a desert all my friends
Were cis until at last I figured out about the internet
And talked a lot to an older lady Ashley I think she was
Who was kind and nice and let me impress her with youthful self-belief
Oh Ashley you were so sweet I pulled the wool right over your eyes
You wrote to me perhaps your time in hell is over now
Like all the trans girls say

La, la-la-la la-la la

I also remember you Melissa living with your dad
Complained you were lonely said she was too afraid to go
Outside she just stayed in did yoga watched the television
I thought I was trying to be your friend and I was a bit but also
I was so busy showing off my hope that I totally ignored the way
You must have felt as if you had no options and as if I did
Like all the trans girls say

La, la-la-la la-la la

I moved to Manchester signed up to mentor young transgender
People in precarious housing what did I think I would achieve
Like Becca oh god you were tall you used to be really good at soccer
I had no idea how to help when you said it was hopeless you were
  broke you were never
Going to pass you got abuse all the time you lost your friends she saw
These visions and joined a pentecostal church and detransitioned
Like all the trans girls say

La, la-la-la la-la la

Then Abby remember we met at the Day of Remembrance so
  skinny and intense
You beat me at pool and we ran all the way to my flat to fuck you used
To shave your entire body every morning for an hour and dilate
For an hour every night you needn't have I swear you're beautiful I liked
Your little scars and tiny breasts you never let me eat in your house
I wanted to love you but you had no use for love like mine at all
Like all the trans girls say

La, la-la-la la-la la

Jo you know those animations you made I think about them all
  the time
Those trans-girl Rapunzels and Cinderellas in filigree moving forests
Of luscious pristine colours just sitting in files on your computer
I wanted to buy some but how do you buy a film where can you put it
I couldn't even properly say how talented I thought you were
I wanted to show you my poems but I didn't the words all stayed inside
Like all the trans girls say

La, la-la-la la-la la

Sophie when we met you still dressed like a boy you barely spoke at all
We'd spend an hour I'd talk you'd say perhaps two things but Sophie
You rode a motorbike you collected samurai swords you acted
So tough but you still got your heart broken so fast you still got raped
By some guy in a bar and I was the one you had to turn to I said
I'd be there for you but I moved to America and fell out of touch
  I'm sorry
Like all the trans girls say

La, la-la-la la-la la

What the fuck with all these missed connections older people
People my age younger people I wanted help so much
I wanted to help why is it so hard to have a conversation
Where we don't lie or sit in silence or feel bad or fight or somehow
All miss the point how can we get better at talking or shutting up
Or whatever it is I need to do and can this ever change?
Like all the trans girls say

La, la-la-la la-la la

I mean it's fine I figured it out by myself and found love
And whatever maybe it made me tough or smart or something useful
But the world is hard on girls like us no joke it really is
And all those years seem like such empty years sometimes I know
They weren't I know I can list all the things I did and why they're good
But it was really lonely so lonely I was lonely all the time
Like all the trans girls say

La, la-la-la la-la la

Enough Of This Oscar Peterson Shit

'I practiced from nine a.m. to noon, took an hour off for lunch,
practiced from one to six in the afternoon, then went to dinner,
and went back to the piano...'

Here I am, I have taken all my clothes
off, I'm creating a nuisance
maybe you should call the police.
Can it be raining? I don't mind if it's raining.
I'd like to meet you and tell you you're beautiful
even though I don't really believe
in beauty as applied to people.
You're beautiful. There.
I have certainly left my bedroom now.

California Encomia

The Road, The Hills
Finding the road is always hard. We're wrong
Then wrong again. I blame the GPS.
We are a car of trannies revving down
The interstate, with bags and bags and bags,
Boxes of books, and half a quart of rum.
We wear our newest, shortest, thrift store dresses,
And play a tune about how hard it is
To be a psycho bitch. We're running late
And driving very fast. Just let the state
Police turn on their sirens, they'll get theirs.
California! You're in a drought.
The olives are all dead the hills are dry.
California! You're mad with thirst
And so are we but maybe it will rain.

Polar Bear
I meant it as a joke. Who plays car games
They read about online? But when the wind
Brings down the longed-for rain at last, I say
'Let's roll the windows down and get undressed.'
And Pythia does. We pause, we glance and then
I do the same, Minerva's driving but
She wriggles off her dress, and Sissy too.
We stare. Like, some of us have had a bunch
Of work (like me) and some just started 'mones,
But there's no judgment, we're just curious.
It's safe. For once! It's like we cast a spell.
Tall girls! Expose yourselves in cars! Pull up
To pee without a stitch to wear! Share
Your nudity and see how long you last.

Truck Stop

Maybe we should be naked. Even so
They seem surprised. I learned to disappear
But lessons get forgotten too and yes
They notice us in packs but let them look,
Sometimes you need to take that risk. Every
Truck stop should have a few of us, stealing
Wasabi peas and telling noisy jokes,
Demanding very complex sandwiches.
We're what I warned myself about, we have
A purpose and a name, we're hungry since
We stayed up getting much too drunk and had
Important conversations where we cried
And yes we're feeling somewhat drained but truck
Stop people we are here to meet your eyes.

The Goddess

I want to praise, but I've been taught critique.
And yes, Minerva can be difficult.
Last night we fought, some stupid argument.
We'd both been drinking, and we know what hurts.
Soft-spoken, scrupulous and measured girl,
All straight blonde hair and pale skin and mouth
That purses when it rests, turned out to be,
Oh right, a warrior. I mean, of course,
We all have had to be. But this was fierce.
This morning, among lemon trees, the sun
Still climbing up the sky, she came
And offered me a way to climb back down.
So praise: this woman's stubborn, sharp of tongue
And eye, she's very kind, and likes a drink.

The Oracle

People think praise is a dishonest mode
But I'm so done with irony. Pythia's
Tattoo says 'pretty worthless vermin' and
Her tits are missiles. She told me she
Can move things with her mind. I half believe
She can. It's like, she always sees your point,
But also past it with such clarity
To what is overlooked, the trash she draws,
The girls like us, the future. All her clothes
Are bright and cheap and way too small, she has
No shame, she finds the use in stuff, which here
Is 'Look it shows my boobs so good'.
She's making cuddly toys do dances on
The dash, and telling us about their lives.

Driving in

Things have to end, there is a traffic jam,
There are palm trees, there is a city here
Of things we have to go and do. It's not
The car. I'd leave the car. But when we pull
Into the parking lot of don't know what
This building is to finish off the rum
And smoke a joint and see if Pythia can
Pick Sissy up and spin her round above
Her head (you know she can) we know that we're
Unknitting, and we do it with regret.
I've never felt like this, so strong, so good,
So clear. I look from face to face, and smile
I never want to turn away again,
Although of course I have somewhere to turn.

Ode To My Breast Implants

I've carried you
Around for years
By now you saline
Sacs

I've covered you
In scar tissue
And watched you
Soften up

And now most nights
You whisper that
The marks don't show
At all

I don't know what
I have become
When you say that
To me

What happened to
That past in which
I used to be
So strange

And wanted to
Become normal
Desperately
Somehow

My heavy breasts
Will you tell me
That I did not
Concede

You are a gift
You always tell
Me what I want
To hear

If only I'd
Turned out to be
Implacable
Like you

Instead I guess
That after all
I'm nothing but
A girl

Grand Hotel

1992

The toilets are very grand.
They have a man in them
To help you wash your hands.
I went in by myself.
The waiters wear bowties
And all of them are French.
The tables are far apart.
The terrace looks onto the Thames.
My dad ordered wine,
'A bottle of Montrachet.'
He told me that it was
The best wine in the world
And I could try a sip.
We toasted to my birthday
But I was embarrassed because
My birthday was last week.
I'm already ten.
This is a grand hotel.
It has big chandeliers
And lots of cutlery
And mirrors everywhere.
The wine is so delicious,
I'll always remember it.
When it's time to order
I talk to the waiter.
I tell him my name is Patrick,
And also about the book
I'm reading at the moment.
I brought it here with me
Just in case there was
Some time for me to read.

It is a historical novel
Called Tristan and Iseult
About a lady who
Lives in a great castle
And is married to one man
But in love with another.
I tell him that it's by
Rosemary Sutcliffe,
One of my favourite authors.
I like her prose style
And I'm interested in the past,
Especially the medieval period.
I ask his advice
On what I should order.
He recommends the chicken
And I say that will be perfect
And thank you very much.
My mum orders the plaice.
Its funny she's having fish
Because on the way here
My parents were teasing me.
They told me we were going
To have fish and chips.
I really believed we were.
But then we pulled up here!
I don't know how they knew
That I really wanted
To go to a grand hotel.
I was very surprised,
Although at first I was
Also a bit disappointed
That it wasn't the Ritz.
But mum says that this one
Has a better restaurant.
I'm wearing my beige jacket

with my denim shirt;
My mum smells of Opium
And looks very beautiful,
She wears silver earrings
In the shape of shells
And dark smoky make-up.
She's dressed all in black.
She handed her cashmere cloak
In at the cloakroom.
She often gets dressed up
And my dad takes her out
To restaurants and parties:
I stay at home.
My grandparents come over,
to look after me.
They live in a council flat
So they like to visit our house.
It's very exciting
That because it's my birthday
I get to go out too.
Mum tells me a story
About the first time
They ever went to a restaurant.
It was after they were married,
When they started to earn
A little bit of money
(They'd once been to Wimpy's
On their first ever date,
But that doesn't count
It's just a burger place.)
My dad asked for steak
And then the waiter asked him
How he wanted it done,
And he asked for it well-done
And the waiter had to tell him

'I'm sorry sir you cannot,
The chef will not allow it,
You will have to have it medium!'
My mum was so embarrased.
Now he orders it rare
And knows which wine to order,
Not that old liebfraumilch
They used to think was good.
The chicken is excellent,
It has been baked in salt
To keep in the juices.
It comes with asparagus
And a white wine and cream sauce.
My dad has a Béarnaise
Which is a kind of sauce
It is ok to have.
My mum says I can't
Have ketchup — I'm allergic,
And also it's too sugary.
My dad's steak is great
And the potatoes are nearly
As good as Irish ones.
Whenever we go back home
He always gets a sack
Of special Irish potatoes
And also Fox's sausages
And Scots Clan toffees
Which you can't get over here.
Then he tells a story
About the very first time
They came to this hotel.
They were very flustered
And nearly turned up late
And were very worried
They'd miss their reservation.

And my mum couldn't manage
To properly finish ironing
The shirt dad was wearing
She just did the front
And told him to wear a jacket.
She said no-one would see.
But then there was a bomb scare
From the IRA
Halfway through the meal
And they had to go out
Onto the river terrace
And it was November
And the wind was freezing
But my mum wouldn't let
My dad take off his jacket
To put round her shoulders
Although she was shivering.
There were some Americans
Over with the army
Who thought this wasn't okay
They said it was a disgrace.
He couldn't tell them why,
Mum kept on whispering
'Patrick, no, leave it'
And pulling at his sleeve.
He almost got in a fight,
Like he used to do.
My dad's name is Patrick,
The same as mine because
We're both the eldest son.
When they take the plates
I say to the waiter
'My compliments to the chef'
Which I read in a book,
The Grand Babylon Hotel,

Is the kind of thing you say.
All the waiters laugh
I don't understand why,
My mum looks worried
But I'm pretty sure they like me.
When we go to leave
They give me a box of chocolates
And tell me that they hope
I will come again.
I feel very special
And it was very glamorous
And now I've had a meal
At a real grand hotel.
By the time we get home
It's almost midnight.
I get into my bed
Which is a four-poster
That my dad hired
A chippie he knows to make.
It's painted different colours
And you get to it up steps
And it's surrounded by swoop curtains
It's kind of like the bed
Out of this yellow book
Of fairytale stories
I liked when I was little.
There was this princess
Who knew if you put
A pea beneath her mattress.
I remember it being made.
The chippie's name is Dessie.
He's not a fast worker
But he always does things right.
Although I think I'd hoped
It would be more like a real one,

Like it shows in the book.
It should be made of oak
And also a double bed
Instead of a single one,
Also Dessie made me
Wardrobes like sentry boxes.
They were dad's idea
But I don't really like them.
Although I'm not a princess
I'm also not a soldier.
But it's an amazing bed
Except sometimes you drop
Books behind the back
And can't get them out.
I remember all the books
I've lost down that crack.
And recite them in my head.
Everyone at school
Is into skateboarding
Or teenage ninja turtles,
But I prefer reading.
They all think I'm strange
And laugh at me a lot,
And tell me that I'm sad,
But I'm not like them.
I want to be special
And I like talking to grown-ups.
I ask if I can read
before I go to sleep,
But mum says it's late
and gives me a goodnight kiss
And turns out the light.
Although I'm very sleepy
I don't sleep for ages
Because I'm too excited.

I went to a grand hotel!
That's a very grown up
Kind of thing to do.
I am ten years old.
Now it won't be long
'Til I'm a grown-up too.

A Prayer To The Sun

Now listen, Sun
Don't you go
Away behind
That stupid cloud.

Shine on me
And I will make
A gift to you
Of half my beer

Poured out on the ground

Glamourpuss, Repent

Precocious child,
bright white trainers,
corduroy trousers
knitted jumper,
nice neat little
polo shirt,
academic prizes.

Glamourpuss, repent!

Skintight purple
velvet flairs,
book of poems,
black v-neck,
furry Cuban
heel boots,
misery and sideburns.

Glamourpuss, repent!

I'm a girl,
I wear foundation,
off the shoulder
hot pink jumper,
floppy hat
hides my face,
always drunk and crying.

Glamourpuss, repent!

Chiffon dress,
purple docs
(I don't care
who stares at me!)
organza ribbon
in a bow,
deep black circles of kohl.

Glamourpuss, repent!

Liquid liner,
long wool coat
knowing affect,
knee length purple
tweedy dress,
drinking gin,
insulting people's taste.

Glamourpuss, repent!

Flirting with boys,
ruffled rayon
mini-skirt,
child's t-shirt,
fitted silk
tail coat,
hammer-toe slingback shoes.

Glamourpuss, repent!

Blue velvet
shortie nightie
hovering just
around my thighs,
guy who's realized
that I'm trans
slamming the door to my flat.

Glamourpuss, repent!

Bodycon dress
I got on sale
nearly fits me,
dangly earrings,
expensive product
in my hair,
food all over my face.

Glamourpuss, repent!

Drinking cider
in the park,
avant-garde
puffy ballgown
teamed with flip-flops
and a hoodie,
I am so empowered.

Glamourpuss, repent!

Dungarees
with orange patches,
leopard-pattern
string bikini,
near-transparent
stripy vest top,
deciding I'm a dyke.

Glamourpuss, repent!

Muscle t-shirt,
golden blazer,
silver necklace
of a grinning skull,
look of horror
when I tell her,
hand-made orange brogues.

Glamourpuss, repent!

Another girl,
says she likes me,
going over
in patent heels,
fancy bra
and suspenders,
on show beneath my trench coat.

Glamourpuss, repent!

Baggy jumper
in several colours,
tights with holes in,
scuffed-up sneakers,
denim jacket,
having all these
unaccustomed political thoughts.

Glamourpuss, repent!

Worrying
about the way that
glamour affects
other people,
sometimes using
'patriarchal'
in my facebook posts.

Glamourpuss, repent!

Walking sandals,
little cardie,
comfy jeans,
pastel top,
lots of worry,
lots of work,
no make-up at all.

Glamourpuss, repent?

Throwing half
of my clothes out,
tears tracking
down my face.
In the bin bag
with these things,
leave the past behind.

Glamourpuss, come back!

Just another
reinvention:
clothes tell people
what you are.
If you change
frequently
you will never be sad.

Glamourpuss, come back!

Glamour isn't
such a power,
barely even
like a spell.
When you learn
your charms are lies
do you cast them anyhow?

Childless Poem

I have nothing. See me stand
Up on two legs. Look at my knees.
My thighs. There's nothing there to see

And that's how choices are.

What Would I Do Without You

When we argue, sometimes it scares me. I don't know how to tell the difference between 'I am very frustrated' and 'Now I will never love you again.'

And you are dramatic. Look how you wave your arms.

What was I when you found me? Bundle of fears and thorns. Rubber band about to snap on every finger. Sack full of jangling things.

Remember I said 'You must only love me if you love me just as a woman, you mustn't love me as trans'? Remember I thought it was ok because (I said) we were both undesirable and that made it fair?

I don't know about your patience. Where did it come from? How long will it last?

You followed me gently. You stood outside my door, your legs a little apart, and said you were already invested. You smiled a lot.

I said I was 'vanilla'. You put things in my bum in expensive hotel rooms and took photos that our friends later accidentally saw. You pressed me up against windows in high rises. You stroked my hair and held my hips. You told me repeatedly, over and over again, that I was beautiful, as if it was no effort at all, as if I must see it too.

You videoed me eating all the pips off a strawberry one by one whilst complaining about contemporary art. You loved this video. You are very strange.

And even now, as you sit at the top of the stairs crying and shouting with your hair in your face and won't look at me or let me take a step nearer, even as you say it will never be the same again, you give a little noisy fart, a way to break the mood, a tiny offer, among all the recriminations. Neither of us acknowledge it, but it's clear.

What would I do without you? Will you ever make me ask?

Damp and Regretful

Well this is bitter fruit, knowledge.
Walking by the estuary
Remembering long ago.
How I was cold towards
People who were kind to me
Preferring those who put me down,
As if rejection offered me
The chance to really be let in.

Worse yet, I always kept
Other trannies at arms length,
Trying to prove I was the best,
Most loved by cis people.
Well, I saw my self in them
And couldn't bear to look at it.
I was cruel and I was proud,
And I told myself that I was kind.

Even now, vanity,
Having to be at the centre of life,
Always demanding to be of use.
Oh my self, look at you:
How you've hated yourself.
You drink a lot, you laugh a lot,
You lie to people all the time.
Maybe you do try your best.

Think of everyone I know
Don't people all have needs?
Don't even I have needs?
So get up again, my soul.
This is the way it goes.
First I loudly accuse
Myself of all kinds of things,
Then I forgive myself.

This is bitter fruit, knowledge:
Spit it out on the ground.
The sky is low and dirty grey:
Birds shelter in the reeds;
Cars roll across the bridge;
The rain falls on us all.
I dry my glasses off
By the dirty water's edge.

Ubi Sunt

www.lynnconway.com/tssuccesses

All these pictures. I guess
I dreamt of being on here
With them. I remember
Being jealous of the pretty ones,
Distancing myself from the ugly ones,
Feeling really fucked up
About whether I counted
As a young transitioner.
It never occurred to me
To write to any of them.
All of these old pictures
Are so uncool and I miss
How terrible it was and how much
Hairspray they all used.
I mean, I used it too.
It was like we were straight,
Just really weird. What happened
To them? All their websites
Are down – the links are broken.
Facebook has swept them away,
Their pixellated gifs
And multicoloured fonts.
Where did these women go,
And who remembers their journeys,
And is there any way
We could still make friends?

Blue Lipstick & Snowfall

You know what's really
Good? To go out the door
Into cold weather
With just a well-
Chosen outfit and a knife.

Thanks and Acknowledgements

I want to thank my family: Sue, Ruairi. And my Dad, long dead as he is: sláinte, Pete! And my Nan: bottoms up, Doll! Thank you all for everything. Look, I wrote a book.

I want to acknowledge some people I learnt things from. This is a book about totally failing to learn anything, but I did have to learn *some* things in order to write it, so:

- My teachers: Peter Cantrell, Rupert Marsh, Tony Nuttall, Mark Griffith, Julie Maxwell, Kasia Boddy, Adam Piette. It was a conservative education I got, but a thorough and a weird one. Thanks, I think. Especially to you, Rupert- I hope you stumble across this slim volume.

- My friends who are writers of literature: Ben Crabstick, Antonia Walford, Athena Thiessen, Jeanne Thornton, Sybil Lamb, Tom Léger, Ryka Aoki, Rachel Pollack. I learn more about writing talking to you than anywhere.

- The poets I've been fortunate enough to edit: Charles Theonia, Lilith Latini, Tyler Vile, Kay Ulanday Barrett, KOKUMQ. You are all geniuses, and watching you work has taught me so much.

- The Trans Poets Workshop NYC: Andy Izenson, Paco Buenasnoches, Vivien Ryder and everyone else who turns up to sit in a brightly-lit conference room and talk about poetry for like three hours every month. Weirdos. I learn a lot from those discussions.

I want to thank those friends and acquaintances and lovers whose lives I took inspiration from, a little here, a little there. Some tiny parts of you are in literature now! Please don't be too angry.

I want to thank Tom Léger a second time, for all his work as a publisher. Tom, you do so much, and I would not be doing this if I hadn't met you. I owe you a beer sometime.

I want to thank Ali, my love. What would I do without you? Certainly not write a book like this.

And finally, I want to thank anybody who reads this book. It is a labour of love. I hope you like it.

xxx

Cat

Julieta Salgado

About The Author

Cat Fitzpatrick literature and politics at Rutgers University – Newark. She is the Poetry Editor at Topside Press, and founded and facilitates the Trans Poets Workshop NYC. She also edits their irregular little magazine, *The Zine Of The Trans Poets Workshop*. Her own zines include *At Least It's Short, I Walked Through The Desert* and *Dances With The Joys Of This World*. She has published poems in places like *Adrienne, Asylum, The Advocate, Glitterwolf, Matrix* and *Vetch*.

About Heliotrope

Heliotrope is a dedicated series of poetry books by transgender authors. We value writing which which tells a story (or several) and is not only beautiful, but useful to its audiences.

In 2016, Heliotrope will publish books by KOKUMỌ, Cat Fitzpatrick and Kay Ulanday Barrett.

Heliotrope is an imprint of Topside Press and is edited by Cat Fitzpatrick. Cat teaches literature at Rutgers University - Newark and organizes the Trans Poets Workshop NYC.

Poets are welcome to join the Trans Poets Workshop- more information at transpoets.com

Submissions of poetry manuscripts are welcome year-round to cat@topsidepress.com

Printed in Great Britain
by Amazon

21916998R00059